KU-034-232

the**people**

the**skills**

the**talk**

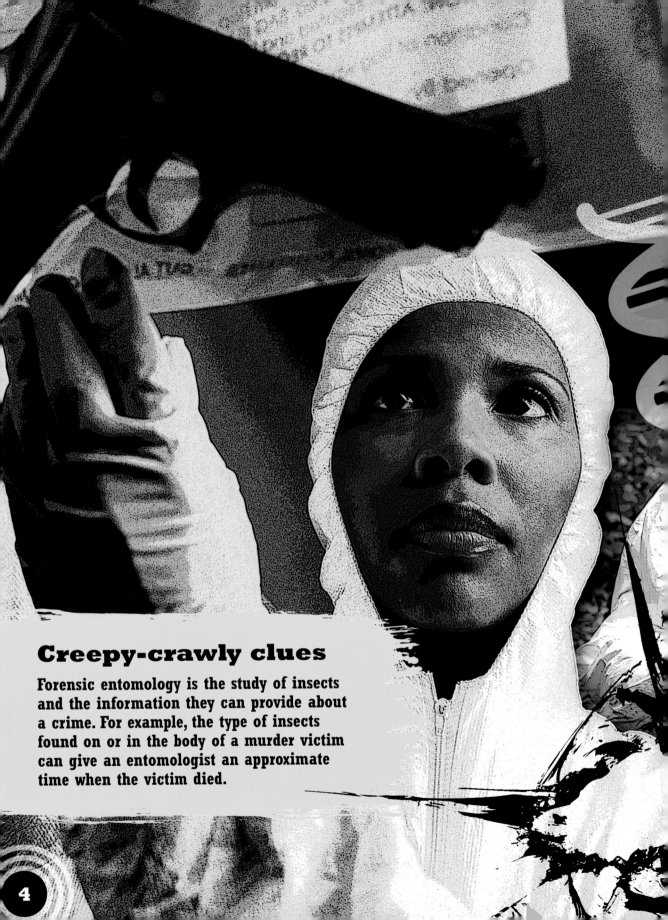

Creepy-crawly clues

Forensic entomology is the study of insects and the information they can provide about a crime. For example, the type of insects found on or in the body of a murder victim can give an entomologist an approximate time when the victim died.

police forensics

Adam Sutherland

Published in 2013 by Wayland

Copyright © Wayland 2013

Wayland
Hachette Children's Books
338 Euston Road
London NW1 3BH

Wayland Australia
Level 17/207 Kent Street
Sydney NSW 2000

All rights reserved

Concept by Joyce Bentley

Commissioned by Debbie Foy and
Rasha Elsaeed

Produced for Wayland by Calcium
Designer: Paul Myerscough
Editor: Sarah Eason

British Library Cataloguing in Publication Data

Police forensics. — (Police and combat)(Radar)
   1. Forensic sciences—Juvenile literature.
   2. Criminal investigation—Juvenile literature.
   I. Series
   363.2'5-dc22

ISBN: 978 0 7502 7744 0

Every effort has been made to clear copyright.
Should there be any inadvertent omission, please
apply to the publisher for rectification.

Printed in China

Wayland is a division of Hachette Children's Books,
an Hachette UK company.

www.hachette.co.uk

Acknowledgements: Corbis: Ocean 4, Sean Justice
20tr; Dreamstime: Andresr 2tl, 7tr, BlueVision 27,
Photowitch 21tr; iStock: Brandom Alms 18–19,
CandyBox Photography 2c, 14–15, EdStock 8–9,
Giorgio Fochesato 8cl, Peter Kim 27l, 30, Mikkel
William Nielsen 24, Jonathan Parry 16bl, David
Waugh 26; Science Photolibrary: Tek Image 9tr, Jim
Varney 28–29; Shutterstock: Aquatic Creature 2–3,
6–17, Arindambanerjee 25, Kevin L Chesson 3br,
21bl, 22bl, Corepics cover, Edw 5l, Fotohunter 2tr,
10–11, Shawn Hempel 21cl, Robert Kneschke 1,
Leigh 22tr, Luxorphoto 2br, 17tr, Loren Rodgers 6–7,
6br, Stocksnapp 26r, Leah-Anne Thompson 17br,
Almog Ziv 22tl; Wikimedia: 12, 13bl, 13tl.

The website addresses (URLs) included in this book were
valid at the time of going to press. However, because of
the nature of the internet, it is possible that some addresses
may have changed, or sites may have changed or
closed down since publication. While the author and
Publisher regret any inconvenience this may cause the
readers, no responsibility for any such changes can be
accepted by either the author or the Publisher.

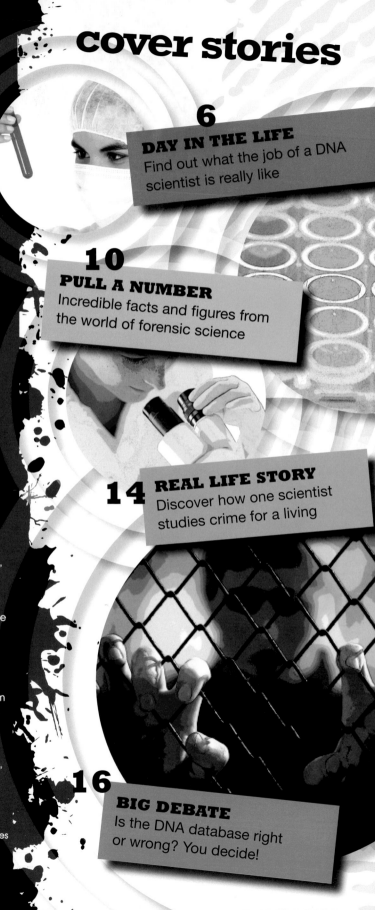

cover stories

CRACKING THE CASE

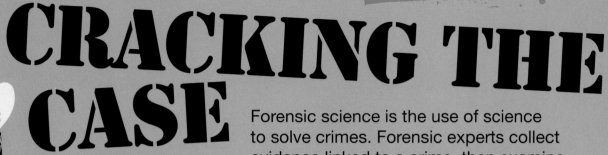

Forensic science is the use of science to solve crimes. Forensic experts collect evidence linked to a crime, then examine it in a laboratory to provide information that helps the police to solve the crime. There are many areas of forensics:

DRUGS AND CRIME

Forensic toxicology is the study of drugs and their effects on the body. By examining a person's blood, urine or hair, it is possible to identify drugs or other toxins that the person may have used or been given by someone else.

THE CRIMINAL MIND

Forensic psychology looks at how and why people commit crimes, and how stress or emotional problems can lead to a person committing a crime.

HOW PEOPLE DIE

Forensic pathology is used to find out how and why a person died. The body is thoroughly examined during an autopsy to try to establish the cause of death.

WRITTEN CLUES

Forensic graphology looks at handwriting and its relation to crime. A graphologist examines a person's writing to find out more about their character and possible behaviour.

TALKING TEETH

Forensic dentistry examines teeth and can be used to identify the victim of a crime or the identity of a criminal who might have been bitten by their victim.

A DNA SCIENTIST ON LIFE IN AND OUT OF THE LAB

DR GEORGINA MEAKIN

THURS JUNE 30, 2012

9am I work at The Forensic Institute in Glasgow, Scotland. Defence solicitors from all over the country come to us when they need evidence in a case. This may involve re-examining old evidence or carrying out new DNA tests. My office hours are 9 to 5, but I have to be flexible. When solicitors are preparing a big court case, they work around the clock, and I have to be available, too. That means weekends and evenings – whatever it takes to get the job done.

10am When I'm given a new case, the first thing I do is request all the case files, plus all the DNA and forensic tests. The laboratory is just ten minutes from my office, so I might walk over there, read through the files and make my own notes. I'm usually back at my desk for lunch.

1pm Sometimes I have to be in the laboratory carrying out DNA tests. At these times, I wear a standard white lab coat, rubber gloves and a facemask to prevent any kind of contamination of evidence. But when I'm back at my desk, I can work on a case on my computer and eat lunch at the same time. You can't contaminate electronic data with a sandwich!

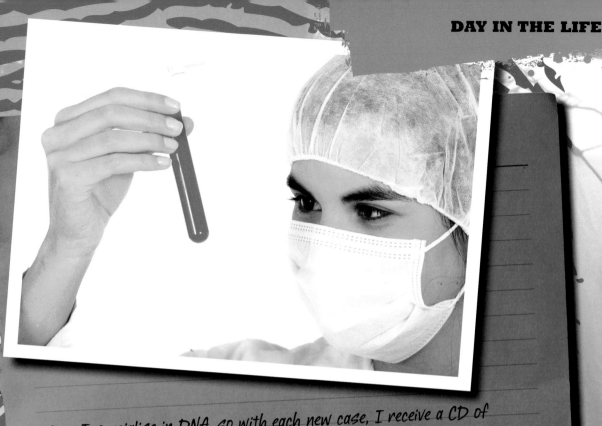

2pm I specialise in DNA, so with each new case, I receive a CD of electronic DNA data. I load this onto a special software programme on my computer that allows me to view the results. We don't analyse a person's entire DNA – that would take weeks – instead we just focus on ten specific areas that are most often different between individuals.

6pm Today I'm setting off for the train station. I have a court case in Birmingham, England, tomorrow morning that could last several days. Attending court is part of my job, so I spend a lot of time in hotels. I'm in court on this occasion as an expert witness. This is a person who provides written evidence and can be asked to give evidence in the witness stand, too. I haven't been in the witness stand yet. Colleagues say it's very stressful, but I'm looking forward to the challenge of it. It's all part of my job after all.

11pm I check my emails one last time before it's time for bed. Court in the morning – I need to be fresh and ready to answer any questions if I'm needed.

EXPERTS ON SITE

When a crime has been committed, a forensics team is sent to the scene as soon as possible to examine and collect evidence that could prove essential to catching the criminal. Success is all about teamwork, and there are lots of people involved, all doing different jobs.

PROTECTING THE SCENE

The police secure the scene. That means not allowing anyone in or out, so that evidence is not damaged. They also record everything that happens at the scene.

IN CHARGE OF THE BODY

The forensic investigator is in charge of a crime scene when a body has been found – for example, in a murder case. He or she is also the person who examines the body at a hospital.

COLLECTING EVIDENCE

Crime scene investigators collect evidence and take it to the lab. They draw and photograph the crime scene, and take measurements so that they can recreate the scene back at the lab.

FINDING THE WEAPON

If a gun has been used, a firearms expert will examine any guns and bullet holes found, collect bullets and shell casings, and search for the tiny amounts of gunpowder residue that are released when a gun is fired.

UNIQUE PRINTS

The latent print examiner studies finger-, palm- and footprints found at a crime scene. They are then compared with the prints from any suspects, prints found at other crime scenes, and checked against a database of prints held on computer.

BACK AT THE LAB

The medical examiner (ME) is the person who decides the cause of death, oversees the analysis of evidence and, if necessary, appears in court to present their findings. The ME also supplies the police with the results of any forensic tests that have been performed.

FORENSIC FIGURES

99.9

The percentage of DNA that is the same in every person.

1835

The first time that forensics was used to match a bullet taken from a victim, with the gun that fired it.

1

The percentage of people in the world with an AB blood type – the rarest blood group.

37

The percentage of people in the world with an O+ blood type, the most common blood group.

1858

The year that the first recorded set of fingerprints was taken by Sir William J Herschel, a British army officer in India.

1,143

The number of unsolved murders in the UK.

1,250

The approximate number of days that medical examiners spent identifying victims of the 9/11 disaster in New York City, USA, in 2001.

80

The percentage of victims that can usually be identified by dental records in an explosion or mass disaster.

All figures provided are from 2010 records.

THE STORY OF CRIME DETECTION

CLASSIC COMICS

FEATURING STORIES BY THE WORLD'S GREATEST AUTHORS

The ADVENTURES of FEB 10, 1947

SHERLOCK HOLMES

by Sir ARTHUR CONAN DOYLE

RACHE

The world famous fictional forensic scientist, Sherlock Holmes, has appeared in novels, comics (above) and many films.

The first forensic scientist was a fictional detective called Sherlock Holmes. Created by Sir Arthur Conan Doyle, a Scottish doctor turned author, Holmes used the science of fingerprinting and blood analysis to solve crimes. In the first Sherlock Holmes novel, *A Study in Scarlet*, published in 1887, Holmes developed a chemical that could tell if a stain was blood or not.

REAL LIFE FORENSICS

Austrian-born Professor Hans Gross was the world's first real life forensic scientist. In 1893, he published the first handbook of forensics. He applied science to crime detection and introduced new areas, such as crime scene photography. In 1901, the biologist Karl Landsteiner first discovered that human blood could be separated into groups, and created the ABO system that is still used today.

THE TRANSFER SYSTEM

In 1910, a French doctor called Edmund Locard realised that everyone constantly picks up and leaves behind traces of their environment – dust, hair, threads from clothes, paint and mud. 'Locard's Exchange Principle' is the reason why all crime scenes are secured as soon as possible.

US CRIME LABS

The first forensics lab in the USA was formed in 1923 by August Vollmer, who worked for the Los Angeles Police Department. The first private forensics lab was created in Chicago, USA, in 1929 as a result of a fight between rival criminal gangs that killed seven men. Calvin Goddard, the forensic scientist in charge of the case, was able to link the killings to Mafia leader Al Capone's gang by identifying exactly which guns had been used. In 1932, Goddard helped the Federal Bureau of Investigation (FBI) to set up a national forensics laboratory, which could investigate cases on behalf of every police force in the USA.

Francis Crick (top) and James Watson (bottom) were awarded a Nobel Prize in 1962 for their contribution to science.

Unique identities

In 1953, two scientists, Francis Crick and James Watson, discovered the structure of DNA. In 1985, scientists discovered that except for some identical twins, each person's DNA is unique. A process called DNA Typing was developed to highlight the differences in each person's DNA. Forensic scientists today are able to take DNA samples from subjects by rubbing a cotton bud on the inside of the person's cheek and storing the information on a worldwide database.

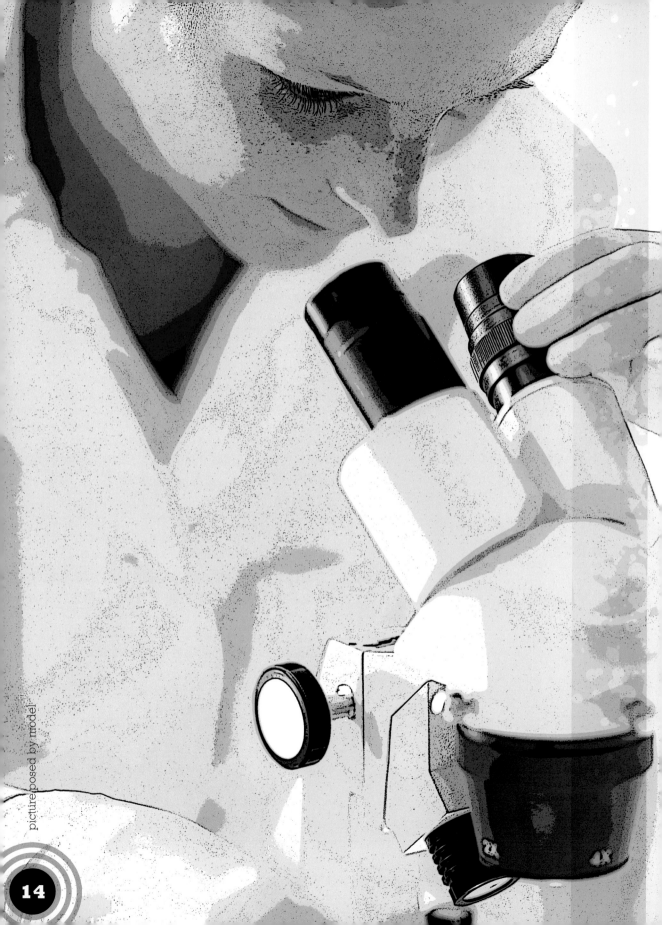

picture posed by model

14

HOOKED ON CSI

MY STORY BY CHRISTINA MARTIN

For as long as I can remember, I really wanted to study law. I loved all the courtroom dramas and CSI-type shows on television and found the legal process of finding and catching criminals fascinating. I decided to be a barrister so that, one day, I would stand up in court and make my case to a jury.

At school, I studied psychology, sociology, English and law. I was planning to study law at university. I really only wanted to study criminal law but that wasn't possible in a law degree. Then my mum suggested forensic science. It was like a lightbulb had been switched on in my head. Of course! Why hadn't I thought of that before?

First, I did a one-year foundation course in sciences. Then I started my degree in forensic science. It was amazing and I loved every minute – even the real autopsy we watched at the university hospital. The sight of blood – or worse – doesn't bother me. We studied everything from pathology to entomology. We even developed our own mock 'crime scene' and gave evidence in a mock 'courtroom', in which we were cross-examined by our lecturers as though it were a real life case.

I've just graduated and so now I'm looking for my first job. I'd love to work as a crime scene investigator, that would be my first choice, but I'm also interested in entomology and ballistics. I'd like to do different things and to have some variety in my work. Right now, I'm spending my days sending out CVs for every single forensic position that comes up. Wish me luck!

C. M

DATABASE FOR ALL?

FOR

Governments around the world hold DNA samples, usually from convicted criminals, which they use to solve crimes. There are calls for these databases to be expanded so that everyone's DNA is included. Supporters say:

1. DNA sampling is an important weapon in the fight against crime. It makes it harder for criminals to get away with their deeds. The more DNA that is held on file, the more crimes will be solved.

2. If you have nothing to hide, then you don't need to be afraid of your DNA being included in a database.

3. The standard DNA test is very reliable. It compares samples in ten different ways – the likelihood of two unrelated people showing the same full DNA profile is one in a billion.

4. 'Familial DNA profiling' – matching DNA profiles between members of the same family – can also help track down criminals. If just one member of a family is on the database, they can all be traced.

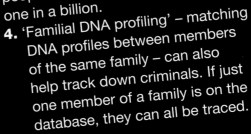

On the other hand, critics believe that DNA testing should not replace standard police work. They argue that:

AGAINST

1. DNA sampling can often provide inconclusive results. There have been thousands of cases of DNA samples found at crime scenes matching several people on a database at the same time.

2. Low copy number (LCN) DNA testing can create a DNA profile from just five or six cells, rather than the usual 200. This can make the DNA test much more unreliable. Many countries, including the USA, do not allow LCN evidence in court, but the UK does.

3. DNA samples can be passed from a guilty person to an innocent person by something as simple as just shaking hands or sitting in the same chair. Therefore, the results of DNA testing cannot be 100 per cent accurate.

4. It is possible for an innocent person's DNA to be planted at a crime scene, either to mislead police or to transfer blame to someone else.

5. DNA testing is expensive, and money is being spent in this area while other areas of police work, such as patrolling high crime areas, are neglected.

Right or wrong?

It's a fact that DNA testing helps to catch criminals. But it shouldn't become the only method that the police use. And it shouldn't mean that everyone in a country should be made to give a DNA sample. New technology and scientific breakthroughs can be brilliant, but people's freedom of choice is also important.

THE TOOLS

At a crime scene, investigators have to discover, collect and protect the evidence they find, then transport it back to the lab. To do this job, they use a wide range of equipment.

plastic tube

TESTING FOR BLOOD

Every crime scene investigator carries a serology kit to test a scene for blood and other fluids that might contain DNA. Light sources (either ultraviolet or infrared) and the chemical luminol, can be used to check for blood traces that are invisible to the naked eye.

EVIDENCE IDENTIFICATION

Date _____
Time _____
Case No _____

Test For
☐ DNA/SEROLOGY
☐ DRUGS
☐ FINGERPRINTS
☐ FIREARMS
☐ IMPRESSIONS
☐ QUESTIONED DOCUMENTS
☐ TOXICOLOGY
☐ TRACE EVIDE▮
☐ OTHER

Description of Evidence _____
Location Collected _____ ☐ Found ☐ Other
☐ Arrest ☐ Seized
Victim/▮
Remark▮
Agency

disposable glove

evidence tag

5

5

Along with gloves, investigators also wear disposable protective clothing, footwear and masks to make sure they do not leave their own clothes, hair and fingerprints at the crime scene.

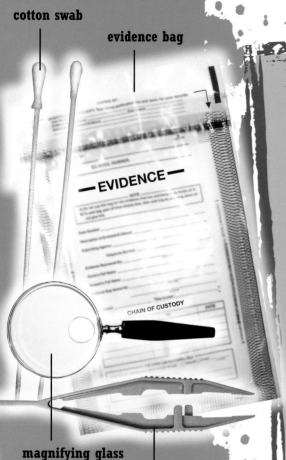

cotton swab

evidence bag

— EVIDENCE —

CHAIN OF CUSTODY

magnifying glass

tweezers

PHOTOGRAPHING THE SCENE

A digital camera is a vital part of a crime scene investigator's kit. Anything and everything is photographed and recorded, from the body to an overturned table or an uneaten meal. These photographs form an important part of the case file, and are often referred to when police are trying to spot clues they might have missed at the scene.

COLLECTING CLUES

To gather evidence, an investigator uses tweezers and cotton swabs for collecting hair, fibre and fluids, and a magnifying glass to spot the smallest trace evidence. Everything is collected in plastic evidence bags and glass or plastic tubes to protect against contamination from outside sources.

DUSTING FOR PRINTS

The fingerprinting kit includes an ink pad, cards to print onto, various dusting powders, an exposing reagent (a chemical that shows up the oils present in fingerprints) and lifting tape for taking prints off surfaces such as door handles, or a body.

MAKING CASTS

The casting kit is used to make moulds. Tyre tracks are called class evidence. This means that they can rule out certain makes but cannot absolutely identify a particular tyre type. However, the tread mark of a shoe can identify its size and manufacturer – useful evidence if police can trace the shoe to a purchase by a particular person.

dusting brush

dusting powder

EVIDENCE!

A crime scene is like a puzzle. Investigators collect the pieces (the evidence) and put them together to solve the crime.

ON TARGET

Investigators rarely find a gun at a crime scene, but they often find bullets that can provide vital information, such as the make and model of the gun that fired them.

BLOODY TYPING

Blood found at crime scenes is examined by serologists. The red blood cells contain proteins called antigens, which determine a person's blood type and can help identify a killer as well as a victim. Antigens are either A or B. Someone with A antigens in their blood is called Type A, someone with B antigens is Type B. People with both antigens are Type AB, and people with none are Type O.

A HEAD START

Hair is often found at crime scenes. If the hair follicle is still attached, it is possible to match the DNA. If not, hair can be examined to see if it contains any chemicals that are not usually found in people, such as poisonous substances.

INVISIBLE EVIDENCE

Fibres from clothes, carpets, and many other sources stick to skin, clothes and hair. These fibres can be identified and matched to try and link the victim and suspect of a crime.

LEAVING PRINTS

If investigators are lucky, they will find fingerprints. These could be patent prints, which are found when a substance, such as blood, is transferred from a suspect's hand onto a surface. Latent prints cannot be seen by the human eye and require special lighting to be examined.

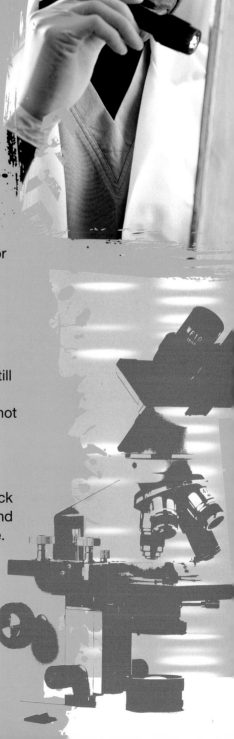

By measuring the dimensions of a bullet hole, scientists can establish the type of gun used.

Scientists test for antigens by mixing blood with Type A and B antibodies. For instance, if blood contains A antigens it will clot when mixed with A antibodies, therefore establishing that a person has Type A blood.

Numbered tags are used to mark where evidence, such as a bullet, is found at a crime scene.

Latent prints can be exposed with ultraviolet light.

Plain whorls look like little whirlpools of ridge lines, and are found in 35 per cent of the world's population.

Radial loops are usually found on a person's index finger. They are less common than ulnar loops.

Just five per cent of the world's population have arch prints.

RECOGNISING FINGERPRINTS

Everyone has a unique set of fingerprints, even identical twins have different fingerprints. There are three main types, with minor variations. This is how to spot them.

IN THE LOOP

The most common type of print is a loop – one or more ridge lines that doubleback on themselves. Loops are found on 60–70 per cent of the world's population. Loops can be divided into two sub-groups: radial loops and ulnar loops. Radial loops flow downwards towards the thumb and ulnar loops flow towards the little finger.

GOING ROUND IN CIRCLES

Whorls are circle-patterned prints that can be divided into four categories:

Plain whorls are the most common, and are either circular (like the rings on a dartboard) or spiral (which become smaller and smaller, like a wound spring).

Central pocket whorls look like a loop with a whorl at the end.

Double whorls include two separate loops that come together to form an 'S' shape.

Accidental whorls are irregular, as the name suggests. Any whorl that does not fit in the three categories above is given this name.

RIDING THE WAVE

Arches are ridge lines that rise in the centre to create the shape of a wave. The arch pattern of fingerprints is the least common of prints and was first recognised only in 1888. There are two groups of arches: tented arches have a higher central rise (like the roof of a house) than plain arches.

FIGHTING CYBER CRIME

Year on year, the number of people who use computers is rising. Not surprisingly, cyber crime is also on the increase. Computer forensic experts are trained to search for evidence that the rest of us do not even know exists.

HIDDEN DATA

Computers can be used for a range of crimes, from hacking (gaining illegal access to someone's computer to steal information), to fraud and even murder! Although many people believe that just pressing the 'delete' key will get rid of evidence forever, that's not true. A computer simply allows you to write over the top of that data, in the same way that you can put another coat of paint on a wall. The original information is still there – and an expert can find it.

THE EVIDENCE

Computer forensic experts look at the hard disk of a suspect's computer and search for clues to the crimes they are supposed to have committed. The information they retrieve helps to piece together the details of a suspect's actions – from the emails they have sent, to the websites they have visited. In 2009,

Crimes organised on the internet, such as terrorist strikes, are increasing every year.

a US woman was arrested on suspicion of murdering her daughter when computer forensic experts discovered that her home computer had been used to search the internet for the word 'chloroform' (a powerful, dangerous drug) 84 times!

STOLEN GOODS

Computer forensic experts also use their skills to find the owners of stolen PCs and laptops. Criminals 'wipe' the hard disk clean, but special software allows experts to recover this hard disk information, providing valuable clues about the real owner of the computer. Because of their specialist knowledge, forensic experts are often required to appear in court as expert witnesses. As cyber crime is on the rise, computer forensics is sure to be a growing area of the profession.

FAMOUS CASES

Radar examines some of the cases throughout history that have made news headlines, and how they were solved by forensic experts.

1. POISONED?

Napoleon Bonaparte was the emperor of France from 1804 to 1815. After losing at the battle of Waterloo, he was exiled and died in prison 1821. While in exile, Napoleon wrote to his friends saying that he was being poisoned. A few strands of his hair survived, and when they were eventually tested in a forensics lab, they showed traces of the poison arsenic. But further research showed that food often contained high levels of arsenic during the time that Napoleon lived, and he actually died of stomach cancer, not poisoning.

2. HAIR EVIDENCE

California-born Scott Peterson was found guilty of murdering his pregnant wife Laci in December 2002. Peterson reported his wife missing on Christmas Eve, and despite nationwide news coverage she was not found. In April 2003, her body was washed ashore on a beach close to San Francisco, where Peterson often went sailing. On his boat, a single hair of Laci's was found in a pair of pliers. Peterson was convicted and at the time of writing is on Death Row.

3. CYBER CRIME

In June 2011, 'cyber detectives' from Scotland Yard's e-crime unit arrested 19-year-old Ryan Cleary on suspicion of computer hacking. The teenager from Essex, UK, is believed to be part of a group of hackers known as LulzSec, who claim to be responsible for the cyber attacks on Sony's PlayStation 3 games system and the CIA's website. At the time of writing, Cleary is awaiting trial and, if found guilty, could be sent to the US to serve his sentence.

4. TELL-TALE FINGERPRINTS

In the USA in 1986, Stella Nickell's husband died of cyanide poisoning. The source was discovered to be a bottle of painkillers, which were contaminated with the poison. However, the police also found traces of a chemical found in fish tanks – like the one in Stella's house. Stella's daughter told the police that her mother had been researching the use of cyanide, and at the local library, two books on poisons revealed traces of Stella's fingerprints! She was found guilty and sentenced to 99 years in prison.

5. FAKE PAPERS

In 1983, the German journalist Gerd Heidemann announced that he had discovered the diaries of Adolf Hitler, the man who led Germany into World War II (1939–1945). The announcement sparked worldwide interest, and the US publication *Newsweek* agreed to buy the diaries for £2.3 million (US$3.74 million). However, when the forensics department of the German police force examined the diaries, they discovered that the ink used to write them had not been available during the war, and the bleach that was used to whiten the paper did not exist until 1954 – nine years after Hitler died. The diaries were fake!

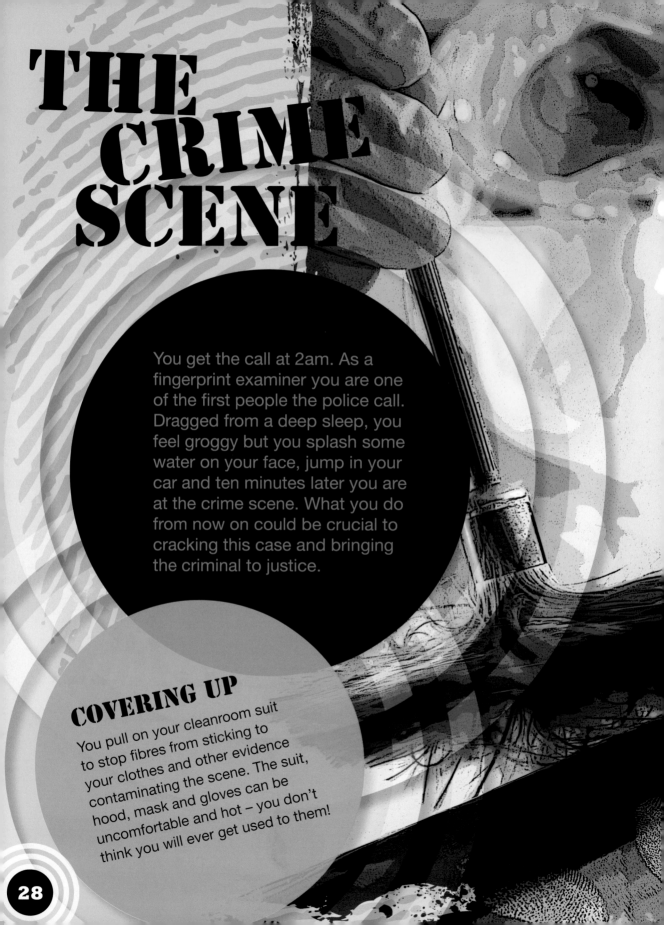

THE CRIME SCENE

You get the call at 2am. As a fingerprint examiner you are one of the first people the police call. Dragged from a deep sleep, you feel groggy but you splash some water on your face, jump in your car and ten minutes later you are at the crime scene. What you do from now on could be crucial to cracking this case and bringing the criminal to justice.

COVERING UP

You pull on your cleanroom suit to stop fibres from sticking to your clothes and other evidence contaminating the scene. The suit, hood, mask and gloves can be uncomfortable and hot – you don't think you will ever get used to them!

FOCUSING ON THE SCENE

You duck under the tape to get to the crime scene. You are the first here – perfect for taking in everything and capturing events in your mind's eye. What happened in this room? Was it murder? An accident? Did the victim know his killer? The answers could be right here, in the evidence all around you.

DOWN TO BUSINESS

You get out your fingerprint kit. The powders come in a range of colours, and you use the one that provides the greatest contrast with the background surface. The walls and woodwork here are white, so you choose black powder. You scan the doorframe and windowsill with your torch to try and pick up any sign of prints. You spot one by the door handle. A wave of excitement rushes over you. It could be the victim's, but with a bit of luck, it might be the killer's! You dust the print, and examine it through a magnifying glass.

VALUABLE EVIDENCE

It is a good quality print. First, your colleague takes a photo of it, then you lift it. You lay a strip of sticky tape over the print, and then gently peel it off. You have done this hundreds of times before but you can still feel the beads of sweat on your forehead. One wrong move and this print will be gone forever. Next, you lay the sticky tape onto a card, transferring the powder and the print. It is done. Now it is back to the lab. Can you get a match on this print, and help find the killer? This is what makes your job so exciting!

CRIME LAB VOCAB

Crack the language of crime scene forensics with the Radar guide.

antigen
the molecules in the body that help the immune system fight disease or repair itself after injury

autopsy
the examination of a body to find out the cause of death

ballistics
exploring the science behind firearms and how they are used in a crime

case files
a collection of information put together by the police and police forensic teams on every crime that is investigated

cleanroom suit
a disposable paper suit worn by crime scene investigators to prevent fibres from their own clothes contaminating a crime scene

contaminate
to bring an outside source, such as extra fingerprints or the fibres from a jacket, into a crime scene. If the outside source mixes with the real evidence, it will confuse results and make it more difficult to find the criminal

crime scene
the place where a crime took place

evidence
any information that can lead to catching a criminal. For example, it could be physical evidence, such as a weapon with fingerprints on it

exposing reagent
a chemical that can be added to a substance to cause a reaction and make something visible that would normally be invisible

gunpowder residue
the small traces of explosive left behind when a gun is fired

hair follicle
the part of the hair that grows under the skin

infrared light
a type of light that can detect heat sources, including skin cells

latent print examiner
a forensic expert who specialises in studying fingerprints

Print examiners check evidence both at the crime scene and within the forensics lab for signs of prints.

latent prints
fingerprints that are usually left by accident and may not be immediately visible to the naked human eye

serologist
someone who specialises in collecting blood and bodily fluid evidence

toxins
poisons that may be present in the body

luminol
a chemical that is used by forensic investigators to detect blood at crime scenes where no blood is visible to the naked eye

serology
the study of blood

shell casings
the outer bullet covering that is left behind when a bullet is fired

trace evidence
the evidence that occurs when two objects touch each other. For example, when two people shake hands, they both collect very small traces of each other's DNA

patent prints
fingerprints that are clear and obvious to the human eye

ultraviolet light
a light that is invisible to the human eye that can cause certain substances, including blood, to become visible

GLOSSARY

database
a computerised list of information that can include people's names, addresses, blood groups and past criminal history

defence solicitors
lawyers who are acting on behalf of the suspect of a crime, rather than the victim of a crime

DNA
short for deoxyribonucleic acid, DNA is the hereditary material in humans and almost all other organisms

exiled
when a person is sent away from his or her home country and is forced to live somewhere else

fictional
not real; made up

fraud
pretending that something is real when it is not

hacking
unauthorised entry into a computer network or website

Mafia
a criminal gang originally from Sicily, Italy

Nobel Prize
a prize awarded to people for their outstanding contribution in their particular field of work. The prize was established by a famous Swedish scientist called Alfred Nobel

recreate
to make a copy of something

scan
to look at something closely

secure
to close off, or not allow entry to a specific area

BE A FORENSIC EXPERT

SURF THE NET

If you really want to get into forensics, clue yourself up with the Radar guide! Start your case by covering the history of fingerprinting, then find out how to classify them!
www.fingerprinting.com

Explore Forensics
Find out everything you ever wanted to know about forensics, from handwriting to handguns:
www.exploreforensics.co.uk

GAMES

The New Scotland Yard Forensics Kit
A must for all crime scene investigators! The kit contains everything you need to examine evidence – and catch criminals!

The Science Museum Fingerprint Kit
Collect fingerprints from your friends and family, and find out how to examine them to find your 'suspect'.

APPS & READS

Follow the trailblazing detective who used forensics to crack cases with *The Adventures of Sherlock Holmes*, available as iPhone and iPad apps:
www.itunes.com

iCSI is a fun game for iPhone and iPad:
www.itunes.com

Police Lab by David Owen (New Burlington Books, 2002)

The Forensics Handbook by Pete Moore (Eye Books, 2004)

INDEX